# HOW TO DOUBLE YOUR CHILD'S SELF-CONFIDENCE IN JUST 30 DAYS

25 THINGS PARENTS CAN DO TO TEACH YOUR CHILD
UNSTOPPABLE SELF-CONFIDENCE

DENNY STRECKER

# CONTENTS

*Foreword*                                                          7

1. TEACH DON'T JUST EXPECT                                          13
   Make Your Bed!                                                   13
   Don't Just Expect Things                                         14
   Assignment #1                                                    15

2. HOW TO MAKE FRIENDS                                              17
   George Hides Behind Mom                                          17
   Friends Are Very Important                                       18
   Assignment #2                                                    21

3. REMIND YOUR CHILD OF PAST VICTORIES
   AND ACCOMPLISHMENTS                                              23
   Don't Give Up Because Of One Bump in The Road                    23
   Past Success Builds Future Confidence                            24
   Assignment #3                                                    26

4. IMPROVEMENT – NOT PERFECTION                                     29
   The Fox and the Grapes                                           29
   Small Things Make a Big Difference                               30
   Assignment #4                                                    31

5. DEVELOP A FAMILY HERITAGE                                        33
   The Bundle of Sticks                                             33
   What Things Does Your Family Do?                                 34
   Assignment #5                                                    34

6. PROVIDE FEEDBACK IN A POSITIVE LOVING
   FASHION                                                          37
   Children Mimic What They See                                     37
   Become the Good Finder For Your Child                            38
   Assignment #6                                                    40

7. TEACH THE VALUE OF TELLING THE TRUTH     43
    The Wise Master     43
    White Lies Are Still Lies     45
    Assignment #7     47

8. TEACH YOUR CHILD TO TAKE PRIDE IN THEIR APPEARANCE     49
    Zig Ziglar On Appearance Counts     49
    Your Appearance Matters     50
    Assignment #8     52

9. AVOID NEGATIVE PEOPLE     55
    The Fox Who Had Lost His Tail     55
    Soar With The Eagles     56
    Assignment #9     58

10. PAINT A BIG PICTURE     61
    The Ant And The Cocoon     61
    The Big Picture     62
    Assignment #10     66

11. RULES AND CONSEQUENCES     67
    The Fox And The Goat     67
    Children Like Rules and Structure - WHAT?     68
    Assignment #11     74

12. YOUR CHILD NEEDS YOUR TIME     77
    The Dog And The Wolf     77
    Quality Time is Crucial     78
    Assignment #12     81

13. FAMILY MEETING     83
    The Two Dogs     83
    The Family Meeting     84
    Assignment #13     85

14. TEACH RESPECT     87
    The Lioness     87
    Be The Role Model of Respect.     88
    Assignment #14     89

15. LEARN SOMETHING NEW     91
    The Widow And The Sheep     91
    Have Your Child Teach You     92
    Assignment #15     93

16. THINKING POSITIVE     95
    The Hunter And The Woodman     95
    Thinking Positive     96
    Assignment #16     99

17. TEACH THE VALUE MONEY     101
    The Two Frogs     101
    Teach The Value of Money     102
    Assignment #17     104

18. LEARN RESPONSIBILITY     105
    The Bat And The Weasels     105
    Assignment #18     109

19. GIVE UNCONDITIONAL LOVE     111
    The Lion And The Three Bulls     111
    Assignment #19     113

20. ACTIVELY LISTEN     115
    The North Wind And The Sun     115
    Assignment #20     117

21. MAKING EVERY EXPERIENCE A LESSON IN
    LEARNING     119
    The Fisherman     119
    Assignment #21     121

22. BECOME AN EXPERT     123
    Hercules And The Wagoner     123
    Be The Expert     124
    Assignment #22     125

23. LEAD A HEALTHY LIFESTYLE     127
    The Ants And the Grasshopper     127
    Healthy Lifestyle     127
    Assignment #23     129

24. GIVE YOUR CHILD CHORES                    131
   The Traveler And His Dog                131
   Your Child Should Have Chores           132
   Assignment #24                          133

25. PUTTING IT ALL TOGETHER                   135
   The Dog And The Shadow                  135
   Where Do I Begin?                       136
   Assignment #25                          137

   *About the Author*                      139

# FOREWORD

Would you like to get free updates and some COOL gifts?

I am constantly working on new skills and adding techniques to my toolkit. You will get it for free when I add something to this book. Just visit:

*http://DennyStrecker.com/confidencebook-bonus*

## ENDORSEMENTS AND ACCOLADES

"Your mentorship has improved Logan's shyness, physical fitness, confidence, and every aspect that karate improves kids. But you also improved me. I learned so much from watching and listening to you. I gained so many techniques on how and what makes Logan tick. You are making me a better father (I didn't think it was possible). Have a great weekend, and thank you!"

### Michael Dyja (Sterling Heights, MI)

"We are so happy Cassie decided to try out Karate! It's been 5 months since she started, and she's gained so much confidence and self-esteem. Cassie has always been and still is the smallest/shortest in her grade and sometimes feels out of place and defeated. Your class has given her a sense of self-worth, and she shines bright every time she sets foot in class. This class has also taught her respect on a deeper level, and as a mom, I'm super impressed with how she will still say "Yes, ma'am!" at home. Lastly, your special dedication to each student and their family is extraordinary- you always greet the whole family with a smile and genuinely care about your students! You pay attention to every detail, from your ultra clean-smelling karate studio to helping families with helpful parenting info (weekly email topics, podcasts, student weekly challenges, and parent night-outs) and creating fun interactive karate instruction!! In our book, you're A#1!!"

### Karri Lido (Troy, Mi.)

"Zach is autistic, and social situations are always a struggle. Karate has pushed Zach far outside his comfort zone. He now has more confidence because of this.

You have been a real blessing to us. You've made a big difference in his life. Thank you."

*Donald Kolosick (Roseville, MI.*

"In the last 2 months, Hunter has been in karate. I have seen such an improvement in his behavior at school and home. This was the Best therapy for him. He had Belt Testing tonight and has already ranked up to a yellow-white belt. He is so proud of himself!!!"

*Kristie Jorah (Madison Heights, Mi.)*

"...I can only say thank you a thousand times to Denny Strecker because more than a business, he cares so much about the kids and always trusts in Keven! Thank you because you believe in Keven and all the kids and help them believe in themselves."

*Doriel Garcia (Pontiac, Mi.)*

"...Dakota was having a lot of problems in school with being able to stay focused, discipline, and some other behavior issues.

The teachers and principal suggested that we take him to see a doctor to possibly medicate him to help him stay on track. As a parent, I do not believe any of us want to medicate our children as a first step to assisting them to 'fix' their issues. We decided to do some research and found that many kids struggling with focus, discipline, and behavior issues were enrolled in Karate. So, as a mom, I did my research and found Denny Strecker.

When Dakota went back to school that fall, we were approached by the principal, who asked us what we did over the summer as everyone immediately noticed the change in Dakota!

Thank you for all your help and everything you do!"

Denise DeGolyer (Sterling Heights, MI.)


## WHY DID I WRITE THIS BOOK?

I wrote this book because, for the past 25 years, I have had parents bring their shy and introverted children struggling with grades at school and having difficulty fitting in and making friends. Week after week, I was able to help each child develop their confidence AND do better in school. Then, I started hearing stories from parents.

"I wish my sister lived closer because her kids NEED your program."

"I have a co-worker at their wit's end with their child, but they live on the other side of town."

I started to hear this more and more, so how can I help the families that need my information but are not in my area? Write a book...!

I want to thank all the people who helped me along the way and to make this book possible:

1 - Melody Shuman is the creator of the SKILLZ program and has mentored me for over 20 years.

2 - All the parents who have enrolled their children in my program over the years have allowed me to work with them

and learn the best way to help their children.

3 - Most of all, to my parents, Ann and Ray Strecker, who have always supported me and been my biggest fan!

## WHY SHOULD YOU READ THIS BOOK

This book will help you...

Become a better parent by teaching you the tools I use daily with great success to help children.

In the next 30 days, your child's confidence will soar with my easy-to-implement techniques. You will feel so much joy watching your child grow and develop that you will be upset that you had not done this sooner. Don't be! These techniques have been reserved for my clients, so you did not know that you knew this stuff. This book will fix that.

Your child will enjoy all the benefits of having confidence and seeing all kinds of doors open to them. When your child has a good level of confidence, they will:

- Be very likable and have plenty of friends
- Be able and willing to face new challenges
- Be willing to take on roles of leadership
- Be happier in their daily life
- Take pride in their accomplishments
- Work harder to earn the things they want
- And so much more....!!!!

Sound like a dream come true? Well, let's get started, and in just 30 short days, you will see what I have seen hundreds of times with the children I work with in my program.

# TEACH DON'T JUST EXPECT

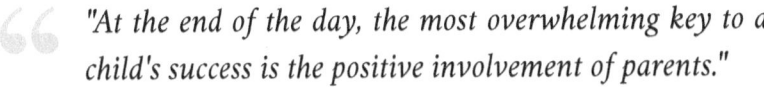

*"At the end of the day, the most overwhelming key to a child's success is the positive involvement of parents."*

— JANE D. HULL

## MAKE YOUR BED!

Carol was the mom of Tommy, one of my seven-year-old Yellow Belts. She was a good mom. She was involved in all of Tommy's activities and made it a point to ask questions to ensure he got everything. Carol was sitting in my office telling me how frustrated she was that Tommy could not make his bed. Her reasoning was, "He is **SEVEN YEARS OLD**! He should know how to make his bed!!" I replied, "Have you ever shown him how to do it?"

## DON'T JUST EXPECT THINGS

As a parent, you need to teach your child how to do anything; you can't just expect them to do it. Watching parents interact with their children day in and day out got me thinking about this issue. Too often, parents expect their children to be able to do something without the proper education on how to do it.

Whenever you start a new job, you always have an orientation. In many instances, when you go to a new school, an orientation gets you acclimated with what will happen, what to expect, and where you are supposed to be. There isn't any orientation for children. The kids grow up, and parents and grandparents expect their children to know many of life's rules. That is not what works. What I hear all the time from parents is,

*"They should know how to do this because they are seven years old."*

There is no correlation between learning a new skill based on age. A child does not know how to make their bed because they are seven years old. They know how to make their bed because you have taught them how to do it – whatever their age!

I want to challenge you with putting an "if" after that "should" and checking to see if you are teaching or are just expecting. At that point, you "should" know that your clothes belong in the dirty clothes basket if I taught you that is where they go. It is not a matter of telling them once; they know how to do it.

The cool part is that this is a universal principle. It applies to adults, your significant others, spouse, co-workers, and children. If you start teaching this concept to your children, it will give them a leg up in the world. Every time you use "should," you can think, "Did I teach them how to do it?" If the answer is, "No, I haven't," then you need to back up and teach them the skill you want to see them do.

One technique I use when working with a child is saying to them, "I'm only going to tell you that 10,000 more times." It is a fun thing that I say to let the child know that I am here to help them. I am your mentor. I am your coach. Please don't feel bad because you forgot; it is my job to remind you.

## ASSIGNMENT #1

Your first assignment is to make a list of things you want your child to be able to do. Once you have that list, review it again and prioritize the most essential items. Finally, pick **ONE**, and work on it for the next month. If we use the making your bed example, it may go something like this:

**Week 1** - Make the bed and have your child

**Week 2** - Make the bed by having your child tell you what to do step by step

**Week 3** - Watch your child make the bed

**Week 4** - Have your child make the bed and have you check it when they believe they did it correctly.

For a podcast that will help you become a Black Belt Parent, visit **http://DennyStrecker.com/confidencebook-bonus**

There are free examples as a bonus for buying my book.

# HOW TO MAKE FRIENDS

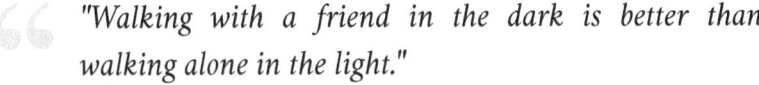

*"Walking with a friend in the dark is better than walking alone in the light."*

— HELEN KELLER

## GEORGE HIDES BEHIND MOM

Terri called me and was incredibly stressed and worried about her son, George. George was a nice and sweet boy but was painfully shy. At six years old, he spoke little to anyone, even extended family members. Terri was afraid that George would suffer from this shyness his whole life. This would impact him negatively in all kinds of ways. I asked her to bring George in to meet him and see how I could help.

It only took a couple of seconds to see what Terri was worried about when I met them. George hid behind her, made no eye contact, and definitely did not have anything to say to me.

We sat down, and I explained to Terri how to work on the Polite Introduction, which would improve his confidence, help him make friends, and open all kinds of doors in his life. Terri and I practiced it a few times, and then she practiced it with George. They left with a great plan in place.

About two weeks later, Terri called and said,

*"You won't believe what happened. Your idea worked! Today, George made a new friend at school and couldn't wait to tell me all about it when he got home!"*

## FRIENDS ARE VERY IMPORTANT

Teaching your child how to make friends is an essential thing in your child's social development. I don't know of anybody who has ever sat down and said, "Here, look, here is a system of five things ..." (which is what I am going to show you in this chapter) "... to help you make friends." Role-play them and put them together with your child. Then they know what to do."

I get parents coming to me saying,

*"My child is so shy. My child goes off onto the side of the playground and sits by themselves. They never interact."*

It just breaks your heart to think that they are going to be alone like that. This will be the best help if you have one of those shy kids.

There are 5 steps to the process I teach my students to complete a Polite Introduction. Each step is essential, so make sure you practice this with your child any chance you get. Don't worry about how well they do it right away. Focus on getting them to learn the steps first. Then, you can work on improvement after they remember each step.

**Step #1 - Look the person in the eye**

It is vital to make eye contact with the person so they know you are interested in speaking with them. I have had kids tell me how their feelings got hurt because they tried to talk with someone and were ignored, or worse, the person walked away. The trouble is, the person was not being mean; they were focusing on something else and did not hear or see that the child was speaking to them. By making sure you make eye contact first, you can eliminate this potential problem.

**Step #2 - Smile!**

It is always amazing to see how many people walk around with a frown or even a scowl all day. No one wants to talk to someone who is in a bad mood. So make sure you smile and let the person know you are friendly and excited to speak with them.

As a special note, you have to practice your smile! I always ask kids to smile, and I see some very scary smiles. The kids look down, scared, or in physical pain. It is essential to teach them how to smile.

**Step #3 - Shake With Your Right Hand**

Teach your child how to shake someone's hand properly. Nothing is worse than a "dead fish" handshake, a limp, weak hand. The "death grip" is just as bad, where you try to squeeze the hand as hard as possible. Kids have to learn that somewhere between these two extremes is what they want to do.

Next, you want to teach your child when is a good time to let go. Have you ever had someone shake your hand for too long? It feels awkward and leaves a " ick " feeling with the person you just met. That is never a goal of what we want people to think after we meet them. Make sure you teach your child this step by practicing it repeatedly.

**BONUS**: Here is a fun history fact for you.

We shake with our right hand because everyone carried a weapon in the old days, and you learned how to use that weapon with your right hand. By offering your weapon hand to someone, you are saying, "I mean you no harm." because you cannot use your weapon if you are shaking their hand.

This is a fun story the kids love to hear in my classes. Now, you can share it with your child, too.

**Step #4 - Introduce Yourself**

The ball is rolling, and your child has started strong. We want them to continue on this solid path, which means introducing themselves in a clear voice. Say, *"Hi, my name is ... What is your name?"*

Have them keep good eye contact and a pleasant smile.

Your child is almost home and has just one more thing to do.

**Step #5 - Listen and Repeat!**

The final step will accomplish two great things for your child. First, it will help anchor the person's name in their mind so they will remember it later. Second, it will show the person that you are paying attention to what they have said and that you care.

Teaching your child this skill alone will give them a great tool, which takes us back to Chapter One about just expecting. Don't expect your child to make friends; be proactive and teach them exactly what to do so they are able and ready to meet people anywhere they go.

ASSIGNMENT #2

Teaching your child a system to introduce themselves will help improve their confidence in many ways. Your assignment is to practice this with your child until they have it down, AND then have them practice it with other people. Have them do a Polite Introduction with your neighbor, Grandma, their school teacher, their friends, and anyone else you see throughout the day.

**Advanced Lesson:** After your child can perform this skill well, ask them questions about the person they met later that day. You can ask things like:

"What was their name?"

"Where did you meet them?"

"What color jacket did they have on?"

"What did you like about them?"

These questions will help them improve their short-term memory, which will benefit them in school AND in life.

For a video that will show you the Polite Introduction and help you become a Black Belt Parent, visit **http://DennyStrecker.com/confidencebook-bonus**

Many free examples are included as a bonus for buying my book.

# REMIND YOUR CHILD OF PAST VICTORIES AND ACCOMPLISHMENTS

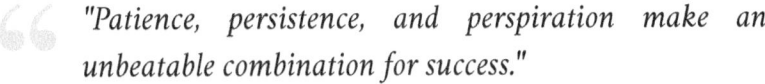

*"Patience, persistence, and perspiration make an unbeatable combination for success."*

— NAPOLEON HILL

## DON'T GIVE UP BECAUSE OF ONE BUMP IN THE ROAD

Maximus is a super kid who has been in my program for several months. He is really kind and very enthusiastic every time I see him. One day in class, he was a little lazy, so I lightly kicked his backside to get him moving quicker, just as I have done with the kids in my class hundreds of times. Well, he did not like that one bit. He decided I was a terrible person, and he did not ever want to come to another class. The grandparents called to tell me about this and then told me about the history behind why this did not go well with him. I understood why Max felt the way he did and explained how I would correct the situation the next time Max came to class.

Max reluctantly returned to class, and I apologized if I hurt his feelings. By the end of class, he was smiling and having fun again, and we were back on track.

Several weeks later,

Max received his new belt. He jumped for joy and screamed, "I did it! I did it!!" as he moved across the classroom floor. I walked with him over to his family, smiled, and said,

*"Aren't you glad you didn't quit that day? Because you never would have had the chance to feel this way and enjoy the success of your hard work."*


## PAST SUCCESS BUILDS FUTURE CONFIDENCE

It is essential to remind your child of past victories and accomplishments. I constantly hear how negative people are and how critical they are when they speak. It is easy to be negative and find the things to pick on if you look for them.

It has become second nature to most people. Almost gone are the days when our parents taught us, "If you don't have anything nice to say, don't say anything at all." It has become the, "You are going to hear what I think of you." It is regrettable, especially when you are dealing with children. Parents forget the impact they have, and the words they choose matter! With children, you want to focus on two things.

First, children are present-minded until at least the age of 12. That means that the only thing that exists for your child is what is right there in front of them right at that moment. They will not remember their past victories or how much they liked to do something in the past. Also, they are not able to picture things in the future.

I can use my martial arts school as a perfect example. If a child is sitting here playing with his best friend, or if they are playing their video game, or watching their favorite cartoon, and a parent comes in and says,

*"Hey, come on. It is time to go to karate."*

It does not matter how much fun that child has had in karate for the past couple of years. They are thinking,

"I don't want to go. I am watching this, or I am doing this." So you start getting resistance at that point. By being able to point to some of their past victories or their past accomplishments,

*"Hey, remember when you got that belt?"*

*"Didn't you feel good reaching your goal?"*

*"Do you remember how you felt when ...?"*

Realizing that kids cannot draw on their past, their mentality still needs to be developed to draw on those past experiences. Being the parent is part of your responsibility. Point those things out to your child and remind them how they feel.

Second, the parent needs to become the "good finder." Again, it is easy to be critical. It is easy to point out the things that you do not like. Think of your role as a parent, mentor, or coach, whatever title you have with a child that you want to be the "good finder."

Instead of saying,

*"These two things were nice, but these four things were bad,"* you ignore the four bad things.

*"Yeah, you did a great job on these two things."*

I often sit down with parents; they are baffled when I speak with them.

Parent: *"Well, my child is misbehaving, A, B, C, D."*

They give me a laundry list of terrible things.

Me: I will ask them, *"What is one good thing?"*

They will stare at me. They cannot think of one. Here I am. I have known the child for an hour, maybe a week, and I can pick four or five good things right off my head.

I have learned that looking for the positive in a situation is a skill. It is not anything that people do. You have to practice this skill to make it better. And continue to practice it until it becomes natural.

## ASSIGNMENT #3

Practice being the biggest cheerleader possible for your child. Look for the ONE thing they do well and celebrate it. Ignore all other things that you did not like. Ignore the temptation to correct or criticize. By celebrating the positive things, your child will want to do more of those positive things, and in time, they will eventually do the whole thing well.

For a video that will show you "good finder" examples and help you become a Black Belt Parent, visit **http://DennyStrecker.com/confidencebook-bonus**

Many free examples are included as a bonus for buying my book.

# 4

# IMPROVEMENT – NOT PERFECTION

*"Have no fear of perfection - you'll never reach it."*

— SALVADOR DALI

## THE FOX AND THE GRAPES

One hot summer's day, a Fox was strolling through an orchard when he came to a bunch of Grapes ripening on a vine trained over a lofty branch. "Just the thing to quench my thirst," quoth he. Drawing back a few paces, he ran and jumped and missed the bunch.

Turning round again with a One, Two, Three, he jumped up, but with no more tremendous success. Again and again, he tried after the tempting morsel but, at last, had to give it up and walked away with his nose in the air, saying: "I am sure they are sour."

It is easy to despise what you cannot get.

## SMALL THINGS MAKE A BIG DIFFERENCE

Now, let's talk about focusing on improvement rather than perfection. Many kids get it in their heads that if they cannot do something perfectly the first time, they will not do it at all. Limiting thinking will create such struggles and problems for the child. What you want to do is focus on improvement - however slight. Your child might be misbehaving six days out of the seven. Instead of looking at those six days, look at the one day. Hey, there was improvement. They used to misbehave all seven days. By focusing on little improvements, you can find the things that worked on that one day and try to repeat those skills or habits every day.

My next challenge for you is to remove the word "No" from your vocabulary. Boy, does this get parents to raise their eyebrows? I am not telling you never to tell your child "no." I am asking that you remove the word "no" from the sentence or your vocabulary altogether. Here is an example.

A seventh-grade girl came home and was very excited. She met a boy who was in high school. He asked her to go to the high school prom.

The parent is sitting here thinking, " Oh my god, my seventh grade wants to go out with a high schooler, and there is no way this will happen.

Naturally, your knee-jerk reaction is going to be, "Absolutely not!!" That ends all conversation between the child and the parent. So, instead, you change that conversation. The mom says, *"Absolutely, you can go once you are in high school."*

Look at that sentence again. She said no but did not have to use the word "no." With our negative culture and our hostile society, this is a massive challenge for all parents. Returning to the beginning, we are looking for something other than perfection but focusing on improvement. I am not saying okay, but by the time you are done reading this book, "no" will be out of your vocabulary. I am saying, though, to start tracking how often you tell your child "no" and see about decreasing it. If you reduce it enough, eventually, you will hit zero, and you will have developed this new skill.

## ASSIGNMENT #4

Start tracking the good things your child does by creating a Success Journal. Every time your child does something "good," write it in the journal. Then, any time they get down on themselves, pull it out and have them read through their past accomplishments.

Part of this assignment is to see how often you use the word "No" many times a day and find creative ways to say it without using it.

For a bonus report, "100 Ways to Positively Reinforce Your Child", visit **http://DennyStrecker.com/confidencebook-bonus**

Many free examples are included as a bonus for buying my book.

# 5

# DEVELOP A FAMILY HERITAGE

 *"Family is not an important thing. It's everything."*

— MICHAEL J. FOX

## THE BUNDLE OF STICKS

After having tried in vain to reconcile them by words, a husbandman who had a quarrelsome family thought he might more readily prevail by an example. So he called his sons and bade them lay a bundle of sticks before him. Then having tied them into a faggot, he told the lads, one after the other, to take it up and break it. They all tried but tried in vain.

Then untying the faggot, he gave them the sticks to break one by one. This they did with the greatest ease. Then said the father, "Thus you, my sons, as long as you remain united, are a match for all your enemies but differ and separate, and you are undone."

## WHAT THINGS DOES YOUR FAMILY DO?

Developing a family heritage is something that has fallen by the wayside. Back in the day, it used to be a big thing for the entire family to go and find their Christmas tree, cut it down, and bring it back to the house. It is something that a small group of people still do today, but most families no longer do it.

Having something that the family does is essential. For example, do you remember those dreaded family vacations? It meant getting in the car and driving across the country to some supposedly "fun" place. You are going to do it because we are family. As much as we hated that trip, we spent time together, which developed stories and a family history.

Find something you can do as a family, then build on it. It can be something simple like a monthly movie night at home, an afternoon at the park, or a trip to get dessert somewhere.

## ASSIGNMENT #5

Develop your family heritage by finding things to do as a family. Make a list of activities each family member finds fun, and then ask the other members if they would enjoy doing that activity, too. The activities with the most votes go to the top of the list.

Start having a family meeting and allowing everyone to speak and tell you about their ideas and wants for the family. This is a great way to give everyone a chance to have a voice in what goes on and to understand what things are "coming up" so they are not surprised or resistant.

For a bonus report, "100 Ways to Positively Reinforce Your Child", visit **http://DennyStrecker.com/confidencebook-bonus**

Many free examples are included as a bonus for buying my book.

# 6

# PROVIDE FEEDBACK IN A POSITIVE LOVING FASHION

*"We must return optimism to our parenting. To focus on the joys, not the hassles; the love, not the disappointments; the common sense, not the complexities."*

— FRED G. GOSMAN

## CHILDREN MIMIC WHAT THEY SEE

I have seen this scenario too many times in my years of teaching. Maybe you have seen it too. Carl was 7 years old and was not the best student in my class. He did not have much focus, had difficulty remembering tasks, had poor communication skills, and could have been better at everything in his life. Carl had been in my karate class for about a year before I ever saw Mom watch a class. When she started watching class, it did not take long to figure out why Carl struggled so much with his confidence. I had started class with the usual warm-up exercises, and suddenly, I heard,

*"You call those push-ups?"*

I was surprised as parents know better than to talk to their children while in class. (It distracts them, so they are not able to focus on what I am saying) A minute later,

*"Come on, you are slowing the class down."* Followed by,

*"You suck."*

**WHAT?!?!** I could not believe a parent would say that to their child, let alone to them while standing in class!!

So, it became instantly clear why Carl had zero confidence. He was beaten down verbally by the person who was supposed to be his biggest cheerleader.

## BECOME THE GOOD FINDER FOR YOUR CHILD

Parents need to provide feedback in a positive, loving fashion. Again, it goes back to the fact that it's easy to be critical; it is easy to be negative. The idea here is always to be that nurturer, a skill that needs to be learned. Parents either don't want to possess this skill, don't know about it, or haven't even thought about it.

You are frustrated, your day has been rough, and your boss has yelled at you, so there is a tendency for everything to roll downhill. So you end up snapping at your spouse, significant other, or kids.

One of the skills I teach my martial arts students to prevent this from happening is to leave them at the door with whatever attitude, negative, or bad feelings they have. One of my students asked me, "Do you mean the karate door or any door?" That was a great question. Why not leave it at any door? You had a bad day at work; you leave it at the door when you walk into your house.

Your house is supposed to be a domicile. It is supposed to be safe. It is the place that you are looking forward to getting to because it is secure. If you don't have that feeling, then by all means, you will have stress in your life, which will add stress to your children's lives.

See what you need to do to change that and make your home your sanctuary. You will find that your life is so incredibly better you will wonder how you ever did without it.

By providing that feedback in a positive, loving manner instead of snapping or, God forbid, using sarcasm when talking to your kids. Parents who do are then shocked when it comes back at them. I shake my head and say, "Well, where do you think they learned it?" The parent stares at me with those blank eyes again. Sarcasm doesn't work. You want to be the nurturer. You want to make every experience a loving, caring one. Positive feedback is best. Another goal would be to remove the word "but" from your vocabulary. Right after "no," remove the word "but."

What I teach is the word "But" is an interjection in the middle of a sentence that says here is what I am thinking, but now here is my excuse, why not? So, an example would be,

*"Hey, can you help me move some of my furniture this weekend?"*

*"I would love to."* And everybody knows what is next.

*"But I've got this to do instead."*

It kills the conversation. People don't remember anything said before the word "but." They need to remember that you wanted to or would like to help. They remember that you were busy. Think about this: if you give your wife or girlfriend a compliment,

*"Hey, that is a nice dress, **BUT** I don't like how it hangs on your hips."*

I can guarantee you she is not going to remember the fact that you said that you liked the dress.

Here is a fun challenge for you to do. Remove the word "but" from your vocabulary.

## ASSIGNMENT #6

It is your responsibility as a parent to be your child's biggest fan. Positive feedback will go a long way to helping them want to learn and experience new things in their life. If they only experience negative feedback, they become shy, introverted, and fearful of anything new. That is no way to live.

Now, I am not saying you can never be negative. I suggest a solid 2 to 1-ratio. For every negative comment you make to your child, make sure you find 2 good ones someplace else.

If you follow this simple formula, you will see your child bloom, grow, and be happy to try new things and experiences.

Would you like to get free updates and some _COOL_ gifts?

I am constantly working on new skills and adding techniques to my toolkit. You will get it for free when I add something to this book. Just visit:

**http://DennyStrecker.com/25thingsbook**

# 7

# TEACH THE VALUE OF TELLING THE TRUTH

*"Whoever is careless with the truth in small matters cannot be trusted with important matters."*

— ALBERT EINSTEIN

## THE WISE MASTER

A teacher once lived with many students in a run-down old school.

The students supported themselves by begging for food in the bustling streets of a nearby town. Some of the students grumbled about their humble living conditions. In response, the old master said one day, "We must repair the walls of this temple. Since we occupy ourselves with study and meditation, there is no time to earn the money we will need. I have thought of a simple solution."

All the students eagerly gathered closer to hear the words of their teacher.

The master said, "Each of you must go into the town and steal goods that can be sold for money. In this way, we can do the good work of repairing our temple."

The students were startled at this suggestion from their wise master. But since they respected him greatly, they assumed he must have good judgment and did not protest.

The wise master said sternly, "In order not to defile our excellent reputation by committing illegal and immoral acts, please be certain to steal when no one is looking. I do not want anyone to be caught."

When the teacher walked away, the students discussed the plan among themselves. "It is wrong to steal," said one. "Why has our wise master asked us to do this?"

Another retorted, "It will allow us to build our temple, which is a good result. "They all agreed that their teacher was wise and just and must have a sensible reason for making such an unusual request. They set out eagerly for the town, promising each other they would not disgrace their school by getting caught. "Be careful," they called to one another. "Do not let anyone see you stealing. "

All the students except one young boy set forth. The wise master approached him and asked, "Why do you stay behind?"

The boy responded, "I cannot follow your instructions to steal where no one will see me. Wherever I go, I am always there watching. My own eyes will see me steal."

The wise master tearfully embraced the boy. "I was just testing the integrity of my students," he said. "You are the only one who has passed the test!"

The boy went on to become a great teacher himself.

## WHITE LIES ARE STILL LIES

Parents need to teach the value of telling the truth. Hopefully, you have already practiced this habit. Little lies are still lies. There is no such thing as a little lie. There is such a thing as a "white lie," but it is still a lie. You can split the hairs all you want.

I did not lie; I just didn't tell you the whole truth - that is a lie.

I didn't lie; I just didn't say anything; that's a lie.

If you allow your child to split hairs like that, then you are setting yourself up for a whole list of problems as they age.

Here is a true story about how some parents think. This is becoming so common it scares me to death. Hannah Montana is one of the Disney characters who was on Nickelodeon until 2011. The TV station held an essay contest, and the winner would receive tickets to her concert. The center of the controversy was that the mother attached a note to the essay saying that the girl's father was in Iraq and was killed over there, so her daughter needed these tickets to get through this traumatic event. It turned out that not only was Dad not killed in Iraq, but Dad was not even a soldier in the military. When the truth came out, there was a significant backlash towards the mom, as you can imagine.

I am shocked that she would go that far. Now the mom, in all this aftermath, was sitting there saying,

*"Well, I don't understand why everybody is so mad. I have had to take my "My Space" page off the internet because I get hate calls or emails. People are calling my house. We had to move. I haven't been able to be at home."*

She is shocked that people are appalled that she lied. She didn't see it as a lie. When the story broke, she told her daughter, "Well, they _said_ we lied, so they didn't give us the tickets." So, even to this day, she denies that she lied. She doesn't see it as a lie.

What message is she teaching her child? That it is okay to lie or justify it in any fashion. So, in turn, the child grows up and believes it is okay to lie.

This goes for everything. You take your kids to the movie; your child is ten years old, and the child ticket is for nine and under. You tell them, "Well, tell them you are nine." <u>That is a lie.</u> You are teaching them at that moment that it is okay to lie.

On the flip side, what comes to mind is that you don't want to double punish your child when they tell the truth. Here is a personal example of what I mean. Our school class went on a field trip when I was a youngster. I lived in Michigan, and we took the train over to Toronto and stayed in a hotel.

This was elementary school, so it was a REALLY, REALLY long time ago. What ended up happening is that we messed around and should have done some things we should have done. What exactly happened isn't critical. It wasn't anything significant, but we got in trouble. There were five or six of us in a room. The other four are the ones who got caught getting into trouble, and they tried to lie about it. I was more intelligent and could hide better, so I did not get into trouble initially. When the other four found out they were in trouble, I stepped forward and said I was also part of the group. I was not innocent. I did this as well.

Well, I got punished just as everybody else who lied about doing anything the whole time. What did that lesson teach me?

It taught me that I might as well try to lie because if I get away with it, I will not get into trouble. If I got caught, I was going to be in trouble anyway.

My point is that if your child does tell the truth, you point that out, and you thank them for being honest. You let them know there is still a consequence because what they did was wrong, but it will not be as severe because they told you the truth about it. So your child is being rewarded for telling the truth, but they are not off the hook for what they did. But never double punish your child for telling you the truth.

## ASSIGNMENT #7

Understanding why children lie will help you deal with various situations in the long run. Steering your child away from the desire to lie is essential to their development. First and fore-most, do your best to walk the talk. Show your child the impor-tance of telling the truth by doing it yourself.

Look for opportunities to have conversations with your child about lying. Watch a television show, cartoon, or movie; when you see someone lying, ask your child what they think. You may just be surprised at the answer you get.

Would you like to get free updates and some _COOL_ gifts?

I am constantly working on new skills and adding techniques to my toolkit. You will get it for free when I add something to this book. Just visit:

**http://DennyStrecker.com/confidencebook-bonus**

# 8

# TEACH YOUR CHILD TO TAKE PRIDE IN THEIR APPEARANCE

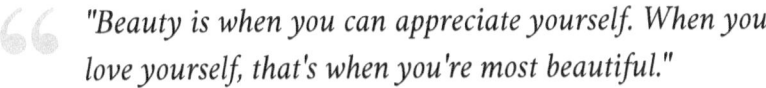

*"Beauty is when you can appreciate yourself. When you love yourself, that's when you're most beautiful."*

— ZOE KRAVITZ

## ZIG ZIGLAR ON APPEARANCE COUNTS

According to a study I read, the way we look has a direct bearing on our paycheck. Employment data from 7,000 adults was analyzed. Interviewers divided the group according to looks and then compared what those working similar jobs in each category were paid. Those who were below average in appearance earned less than those rated "average." Those rated average earned less than those placed "above average."

Appearance includes many things. The style and neatness of your clothing, the shine on your shoes, the crease in your shirt, your choice of colors, and many other things affect your "appearance rating." How you fix your hair, your make-up, and all the elements of your personal grooming contribute.

However, the most significant factor is the smile on your face, followed closely by your attitude and sense of humor. A good sense of humor and a positive attitude are vital as you move into the upper echelons of business. The reality is that people promote people. Evidence is solid that when everything else is equal, we will promote the person we like versus the one about whom we might feel either neutral or negative, regardless of their skills.

The question is, who do we like? You will agree that the people who are pleasant, cheerful, and optimistic are easier to like than those inclined to be dour and even negative in their approach to life. It's also true that the positive, happy person will get more done and cooperate more with their fellow workers than the negative individual. It is a practical matter that employers seek those who "fit," get more done, and are pleasant to be around.

So, let your "Sunday best" appearance include a smile, a great attitude, and an easy sense of humor. Try it, and I'll bet you, too, will join the "above average" ranks in salary and success in life.

## YOUR APPEARANCE MATTERS

Teach your child to take pride in their appearance. Again, for the sake of conversation, you see the kids these days walking around. Their hair is not cut. You see the long, shaggy hair. It's not combed. It's not groomed. The pants hang halfway down so you can see their underwear, which is a fashion statement.

I am still waiting to see the true essence of the fashion statement that way. Again, you have got some schools that require uniforms, ties, and suits. You don't need to go that far but teach your child to take pride. They should want to shower because nobody likes to be around somebody who smells.

Parents should give them some leeway about hair. It doesn't have to be the military haircut, straight at an inch and a half. You certainly want to have some freedom but take pride in exactly what that is and, at the same time, set some standards. I hear parents negotiating with their kids about cutting their hair. If it is not acceptable the way it is, then they have to fix it. Tell them this is the way it is, period.

You can do whatever you want, but you have to be able to follow these guidelines. Teaching them to take pride in their appearance will make them feel better about themselves in the long run. It is natural that if you wear those Sunday clothes to church, everybody feels better when they are dressed up. You may not feel comfortable, but you look better, so you feel better.

In the past, I was a "karate bum." I always wore sweatpants to school. When I got to school, I changed into my karate uniform. That was comfortable. However, I found that people should have taken me more seriously as an educator or a business person.

Once we started doing these different events, I went out and bought a nice suit and wore it to a family function a week later. Everybody was just in awe that I got dressed for the event. So that taught me right there that I should be taking pride in how I look and dress. It is that important.

Now granted, you can always go to the far end, too. You don't have to have super expensive designer clothes for everything. That is not what I am saying. It is just a matter of taking pride in looking your best in what you are comfortable wearing.

## ASSIGNMENT #8

Teaching your child to take pride in their appearance and things is something only some parents think about very often. We all know that people like to make judgments without all the information, so if you look a certain way, you are very likely to be treated that way. So why stack the deck in your child's favor by teaching them to pay attention to how they look?

It is also a crucial trait to learn so they will take good care of their things as they get older. Children who don't care about their things tend to have trouble as they age because their "things" become more extensive and expensive. What happens if you don't care for your car or house? Neglect it for too long, and something significant will cause it to break or fall apart.

Would you like to get free updates and some _COOL_ gifts?

I am constantly working on new skills and adding techniques to my toolkit. You will get it for free when I add something to this book. Just visit:

**http://DennyStrecker.com/confidencebook-bonus**

# 9

# AVOID NEGATIVE PEOPLE

 *"You cannot have a positive life and a negative mind."*

— JOYCE MEYER

## THE FOX WHO HAD LOST HIS TAIL

A FOX caught in a trap escaped but, in so doing, lost his tail.

After that, feeling his life a burden from the shame and ridicule to which he was exposed, he schemed to convince all the other Foxes that being tailless was much more attractive, thus making up for his deprivation. He assembled many Foxes and publicly advised them to cut off their tails, saying that they would not only look much better without them but would get rid of the weight of the brush, which was a great inconvenience.

One of them interrupted him and said, "If you had not yourself lost your tail, my friend, you would not thus counsel us."

## SOAR WITH THE EAGLES

Avoiding negative people is a big challenge since so many are worldwide. If you are around negative people all the time, it can bring your attitude down. It can make you harmful. I use the example of the overweight women's bowling team. One of the ladies on the team decides,

"I want to feel better about myself; I'm going to look better. I'm going to lose some weight."

She starts to lose a couple of pounds. Do all of the other ladies on the bowling team say,

"Great job. You are doing awesome. You look so much better?"

No. Usually, what happens is the women start to say things like,

"Why are you dieting?"

"You look good the way you are. You don't need to do that."

What tends to happen when trying to better yourself is that everybody else starts to feel jealous, some consciously and others subconsciously. So what they do is they try to pull you back down with the group.

This is an excellent skill for adults, especially as a skill to pass on to your children. Anytime you try to set yourself apart, people will try to drag you down because they are jealous. Sometimes, this jealousy is direct and immediate. Other times, it is a little sneakier. People tend to get comfortable with themselves, and anything (or anyone) who comes along and disrupts that comfort is a problem. People dislike feeling uncomfortable, so they attack the thing until it disappears.

For example, what do we say about the one kid in school who had all the answers to the teacher's questions?

"What a brown noser."

If you remember that time in elementary school, we were jealous because someone else had the answers. Of course, being kids then, we made fun of the one who answered.

If you see that your child's friends are negative, then it is time to step in and say,

"It's time to find some new friends."

Go back to those five skills I gave you for making friends, and use them to find a better set of friends. One of the big ideas I am trying to develop in my martial arts school is the sense of community. In the old days, it took a village to raise a child, and these days, we don't want the town anywhere near our kids. It is a real shame and loss for everybody that this idea is fading in our culture.

What I do in the martial arts school is just that. We have one martial arts team, and every student, parent, and sibling of a student in the school is part of the team. Everybody belongs, everybody plays, everybody gets along. You may not like somebody else on the team, but you will be respectful and get ahead.

It is always a positive mindset that I stress to the children. When people walk in the door, that is what I constantly hear,

"I like coming to this school because I forget about everything else bad that has happened that day."

That is what I focus on - making every visit a happy experience. The easiest way to do that is to avoid negative people that I call time vampires. People are going to sit, and they are going to want to tell you what is going on in their lives and how bad it is so that you feel sorry for them. Make it a point not to listen.

"Hey, I don't have time for this. I've got to go do my thing and be focused on the positive."

Start with yourself, and then spread it to your kids. It will be pleasantly surprised how much better your home begins to feel and how much more you want to be there.


## ASSIGNMENT #9

Teaching your child how to avoid negative people in their life will save them decades of grief. Nothing is worse than getting sucked into someone else's vortex of "poor me" stories that have no solution because the person does not want one. Believe it or not, some people only seem to be happy when they are miserable. How crazy is that?

The adage that misery loves company is true. It takes work to cut out and avoid such negativity, but I guarantee you that you will enjoy your life much more once you do.

Would you like to get free updates and some _COOL_ gifts?

I am constantly working on new skills and adding techniques to my toolkit. You will get it for free when I add something to this book. Just visit:

**http://DennyStrecker.com/confidencebook-bonus**

# PAINT A BIG PICTURE

> "*All successful people, men and women, are big dreamers. They imagine what their future could be, ideal in every respect, and then they work every day toward their distant vision, that goal or purpose.*"
>
> — BRIAN TRACY

## THE ANT AND THE COCOON

An Ant nimbly running about in the sunshine for food came across a Cocoon near its time of change. The Cocoon moved its tail and thus attracted the attention of the Ant, who then saw for the first time that it was alive. "Poor, pitiable animal!" cried the Ant disdainfully. "What a sad fate is yours! While I can run hither and thither, at my pleasure, and, if I wish, ascend the tallest tree, you lie imprisoned here in your shell, with power only to move a joint or two of your scaly tail." The Cocoon heard all this but did not try to make any reply.

A few days after, when the Ant passed that way again, nothing but the shell remained. Wondering what had become of its contents, he felt himself suddenly shaded and fanned by the gorgeous wings of a beautiful Butterfly. "Behold in me," said the Butterfly, "your much-pitied friend! Boast now of your powers to run and climb as long as you can get me to listen." So saying, the Butterfly rose in the air and, borne along and aloft on the summer breeze, was soon lost to the sight of the Ant forever.

## THE BIG PICTURE

It is amazing to me, working with kids day in and day out, that they don't have any goal-setting skills. Thinking back to Chapter One, it is because parents expect it.

Think about it: have you honestly ever sat down and taught your child how to set a goal? Not only that but how do you check up on it and adjust it? Then, once the goal is accomplished, how do we set another one?

What I have started to do with all of the kids that I work with now is to say to them,

"You always have to have five goals that you are actively working on, and they have to be written down."

That is one of the five aspects of a goal. It has to be written down. This step alone has got the kids to think. Of course, the first several months you do this with your child will be fundamental and sloppy. But again, we are not looking for perfection; we are moving towards improvement. So I encourage you to do this with your kids. Ask them,

*"What is it you want?"*

*"Well, I want to earn an A in this class."*

*"Okay, well, what must you do to do that?"*

*"Well, I've got to get A's on my quizzes."*

*"When are your quizzes?"*

*"Okay, so you're going to study here, and here, and here."*

Sit down and do this with them. Take them through the process step by step, over and over and over again, until they can show you they can do it without your help.

Then you know what you do? You check on them anyway.

Check-in and follow up every so often with them. You kind of check-in, "Hey, great, yep, still going." It is a matter of managing what you expect now that you have been taught this habit. This is one of Steven Covey's "Seven Habits of Highly Effective People."

Your second task in this chapter is to create a journal. I am surprised by the lack of writing skills kids have these days. I started giving the kids some brain teasers that they could write out. I watched kids take over 30 minutes to write four short sentences. This just shocked me. We expect writing skills, but they need to be taught. So let's put something in place that will help them with that.

Creating a journal, I found, has done that. By just writing in what your child is expected to do tomorrow, next week, in another month, or what they did do today, what did they accomplish? This is also going to allow you to thumb through the journal in six months and say,

*"Hey, you remember that. Wasn't that neat?"*

It will give you that information to return to those good times and remember those victories. What I love about this process is that it is not limited to kids.

If you do not have a journal that you are writing in, get started on one. Use it when feeling down so you have something to look back at to remember that you are a good parent.

I get phone calls or emails saying, "I'm the worst parent in the world. I suck as a parent. I'm doing everything wrong." The trigger was usually your significant other or spouse just beat you up over something that you did or didn't do, or the kids were sitting there in your face telling you, "I hate you." Look in your journal and find your victories.

I have sat down with many mothers and watched the heart-break in their eyes as they are being told by their child that, *"I hate you."* If you have your journal, those are the times you can dig, look back, and reaffirm, "Hey, I am not, and I'm not a bad parent."

You can read and remember, *"I have done these things."*

It can beat that negative cycle.

If there is a significant goal, your final step is to break it down into smaller steps. So take a little time instead of trying to chunk one huge thing, "Hey, I've got this book report, and it is due in three weeks. go." Break it up into little things.

When are you going to have the reading part of it done? When are you going to have the research done?

When are you going to have the outline done?

Do it if you need to break it down more minor than that.

It doesn't matter how many steps it takes to succeed.

It is a matter of you having to take those steps.

One of the most remarkable skills a parent has (as I'm sure everybody is reading this book) is patience. Once you lose your patience, then all learning stops. As soon as you get angry, start lecturing, or start yelling, all learning stops. So that is another bonus for you here. Even under extreme circumstances, you should try to never yell at your kids. Think about when we were kids. As soon as my mom started yelling, click. I would turn right off thinking,

*"Yep, here she goes again. She will rant for about three or four minutes, and then I can be about my way."*

So make it a goal not to keep your cool and to be able to be patient with them, and treat this as a good learning experience for them. Of course, there are those times when all else has failed, and you may lose your cool. That is okay, too. Please do your best to make it the exception, not the general rule.

## ASSIGNMENT #10

Being able to see the Big Picture will help your child in a variety of ways as they grow up. Being able to set goals and know how to achieve them will give them a significant advantage over the majority of children their age. Most kids float through life. Help your child build a path to where they want to go, and they will get to places they never dreamed they could. But it would help if you had a plan, or they will never reach their full potential.

Would you like to get free updates and some _COOL_ gifts?

I am constantly working on new skills and adding techniques to my toolkit. You will get it for free when I add something to this book. Just visit:

**http://DennyStrecker.com/confidencebook-bonus**

# RULES AND CONSEQUENCES

*"You gain strength, courage, and confidence by every experience in which you stop to look fear in the face. You are able to say to yourself, 'I lived through this horror. I can take the next thing that comes along."*

— ELEANOR ROOSEVELT

## THE FOX AND THE GOAT

One day, a fox fell into a deep well and could find no means of escape. A Goat, overcome with thirst, came to the same well and, seeing the Fox, inquired if the water was good. Concealing his sad plight under a merry guise, the Fox indulged in lavish praise of the water, saying it was excellent beyond measure and encouraging him to descend. The Goat, mindful only of his thirst, thoughtlessly jumped down. Still, just as he drank, the Fox informed him of the difficulty they were both in and suggested a scheme for their common escape. "If," said he, "you will place your forefeet upon the wall and bend your head, I will run up your back and escape and will help you out afterward." The Goat readily assented, and the Fox leaped upon his back. Steadying himself with the Goat's horns, he safely reached the mouth of the well and made off as fast as he could. When the Goat upbraided him for breaking his promise, he turned around and cried out, "You foolish old fellow! If you had as many brains in your head as you have hairs in your beard, you would never have gone down before you had inspected the way up, nor have you exposed yourself to dangers you could not escape.

## CHILDREN LIKE RULES AND STRUCTURE - WHAT?

Rules and consequences come into play because parents must set boundaries for their kids. Rules generally are relatively easy for parents. On occasion, there is one parent who doesn't like to have rules or enforce them. Then, the other parent is forced to play the bad cop all the time. This is a topic for another time.

The biggest thing you have to ensure is that consequences for bad behavior are in place. Whenever I talk to parents about an issue or a challenge that they are having, that is what I find the majority of the time. There are no consequences, and the parent is frustrated trying to figure out why the rule isn't working. It is pretty straightforward; it is because there are no consequences. My father always says,

*"If there are no consequences for bad behavior, bad behavior will continue."*

Some of the guidelines to know are:

#1 - the consequence has to be clear

#2 - it has to be understood by the child

#3 - it must be known before the rule is broken.

Otherwise, it is just punishment, and anytime that you are just punishing your child, that is not necessarily fair. Here is an example for you:

Your boss walks up to your desk and says,

*"Hey, you forgot to do this. I'm going to dock you one week's pay,"*

You say, *"Well, you never told me to do that."*

*"Well, it doesn't matter; you're supposed to know."*

You would feel pretty upset. Well, a lot of times, that is how parents approach raising their children, and that same process should ensure clear consequences. In short, if you do A, B is going to happen.

I have worked a lot with parents (it seems like spring fever is setting in, and the kids are testing the waters and acting more.) One example would be,

*"My child kept touching another child at school. The teacher told him to stop it, but he looked right at the teacher and touched the other child again. He knew he wasn't supposed to be doing it; he knew that he was going to get in trouble for it, but he just didn't care."*

When ed the parent is right there,

*"Okay, so what happened?"*

The parent said, *"Well, what do you mean? He got in trouble."*

*"Okay. Well, what happened?"*

*"Well, he got put on yellow."*

They have a color coding system at this particular school, and so what I said was,

*"Okay, well, there wasn't any real consequence to his behavior."*

He broke a rule, so it should be,

*"Johnny, if you touch anyone again, then you are going to have to sit out of recess, and you won't be able to go outside, or you won't be able to play."*

At that point, you have a clear consequence, and now the child can decide how they will behave.

Here is a common mistake parents make. They try to control the person, and that never works. Again, apply it back to yourself in your work environment. Anytime somebody tries to control you, your natural reaction is to rebel. Well, kids are no different.

Instead of trying to control the person, you always want to stop the bad behavior or get the child to behave in the positive way you want. That is why you say something like,

*"If you do this again, this is what will happen."*

By saying that, you are allowing the child to decide on their subsequent behavior; they get to make the choice. Change the behavior, and all will be well. Don't change the behavior and receive the consequence.

The child knows exactly what will happen one way or the other. If they don't do it again, that is the rule, and we will be able to move forward and do fun things. If they choose to do it again, you have to ensure a consequence is in place. Right next to the consequences of finishing up this topic is consistency.

I hear from parents all the time,

*"Well, I even put the rules in place, but my spouse doesn't follow along, or they don't agree with them or back me."*

That is a challenging situation. There is no simple answer to this issue. You have to figure out a plan that works for your family or ask your spouse not to interfere.

Let's continue with the idea of consistency. If you are not consistent, then the kids will not know if the rules apply. An excellent example of this is when the kids run up and say,

*"Mom. Mom. Mom. Mom. Mom. Mom. Mom. Mom,"* and they go on and on. Finally, after about the 12th time, the parent says, *"What?!"* and then listens to the child and answers them.

Instead, you should stop the situation. You look at your child and you say,

*"I'm talking to somebody. You are being rude. You need to wait until I am done, and I will happily give you my full attention."*

This teaches them patience and respect.

Another point that I generally add is that when a child approaches, they should raise their hand to speak to you instead of just talking repeatedly.

The same thing goes with the word "no." If your child asks you to do something, you say "no."

Again, I see this day after day, and it kills me.

*"Mom, can I have this?"*

*"No."*

*"Can I have it, please?"*

*"No."*

*"Can I have it, please?"*

*"No."*

*"Can I have it please please please?"*

*"Well, okay here."*

What you have just taught your child is this,

If mom says no, it doesn't mean no. If I ask five times, I can get to a yes.

What I always try to put in place is elevated consequences.

I have no problem with a child asking for something. That is part of life, and that is growing up, and that is what we want, that communication.

*"Mom, can I have this?"*

*"No."*

*"Mom, can I have this?"*

*"Okay, I said no once, and if you ask me again, you will have to go to bed 10 minutes early tonight."*

However, you want to set it up. At that point, you have elevated their risk, so again, you are controlling the behavior, not the person.

They have to decide how badly they want whatever it is. If they know if they ask again, the answer will be no, and there will be a penalty attached to it, they are less likely to ask again.

It has never happened that I have had to go to the next stage and offer another penalty because as soon as I institute the first one, they see that I mean business and that I am serious, and that takes care of the whole issue.

Now, doing this once, will it take care of everything? Not. That is another thing that I hear a lot from parents,

*"My child is 12 years old; they should be able to clean their room."*

Right away, you are going to hear back from me,

*"Well, only if you have taught them that particular skill."*

Just because a child is however many years old, it doesn't automatically equate to being able to have a particular skill. We have got to teach them a skill just like right now. I am teaching you a parenting skill, and it doesn't matter if you are a 25-year-old parent, a 50-year-old parent, or even a grandparent. These skills will still apply, but I expect you to know them once I have taught them.

Are you one of those parents who say,

*"We don't have rules for our kids. They are self-guided."*

That is not being a parent. Part of a parent's responsibility is to set up boundaries, and anybody who tells you their child does better without rules is delusional. I will say that to their face, I will say it to your face, I will say it publicly, and I will say it privately.

**If you do not have rules and boundaries for kids, you are headed down a path of serious trouble for a long time.**

ASSIGNMENT #11

Create a list of destructive behaviors and then add a consequence next to each one. Go over this list with your child and post it on the refrigerator. Any time your child misbehaves, go to the list, remind them of the consequence, and enforce it. This will eliminate most whining and complaining because the child knows about the list, and you are just implementing it.

Would you like to get free updates and some _COOL_ gifts?

I am constantly working on new skills and adding techniques to my toolkit. You will get it for free when I add something to this book. Just visit:

**http://DennyStrecker.com/confidencebook-bonus**

# YOUR CHILD NEEDS YOUR TIME

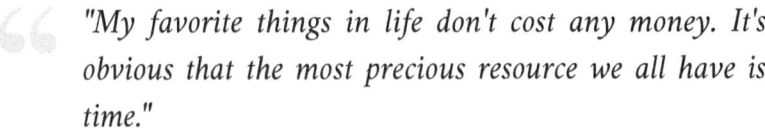

*"My favorite things in life don't cost any money. It's obvious that the most precious resource we all have is time."*

— STEVE JOBS

## THE DOG AND THE WOLF

A gaunt wolf was almost dead from hunger when he happened to meet a house dog who was passing by. "Ah, Cousin," said the Dog.

"I knew how it would be; your irregular life will soon ruin you. Why do you not work steadily as I do and get your food regularly given to you?"

"I would have no objection," said the Wolf, "if I could only

get a place."

"I will easily arrange that for you," said the Dog; "come with me to my master, and you shall share my work."

So the Wolf and the Dog went towards the town together. On the way there, the Wolf noticed that the hair on a specific part of the Dog's neck was very much worn away, so he asked him how that had come about.

"Oh, it is nothing," said the Dog. "That is only the place

where the collar is put on at night to keep me chained up; it

chafes a bit, but one soon gets used to it."

"Is that all?" said the Wolf. "Then good-bye to you, Master

Dog."


## QUALITY TIME IS CRUCIAL

Three different areas of quality time need to be considered. The first and foremost is family time. "Quality" is the key word - Quality time. Time is a tricky commodity for a lot of people. It is one of the critical things I work on with the kids in my program. I speak to my classes about Time Management just about every week. Managing your time so you get more done within the set workday, the week, or the length of time.

You probably know someone who is notoriously late for every-thing they do. I see it at my school too. If I have a class at 6:00, some parents walk in at 5:00 or 10 a.m. Then, if I move the class to 6:30, they will still walk five or 10 minutes late. They need to learn how to manage their time well.

To have quality time for your family, don't think of it as,

*"We have got to set out a whole afternoon for this to work."*

Instead, it can be as simple as:

*"Hey, every 10 minutes before bedtime, we are going to sit down and read a book,"* if reading is what your child likes to do or if that is what you want to do with your child.

It could be watching a family TV show, going for a walk, or any particular event as long as the quality part of that equation is ensuring your child has 100% of your attention. You don't take your cell phone, you don't have any other distractions, you turn the phone off if you have to in the house, put down your iPhone if you are into technology. Facebook will not disappear if you stop posting for an hour. Candy Crush or any other time vampire game will be fine if you last played it a while ago.

The world won't end if you disconnect or unplug for 15 or 30 minutes a night to spend time with your family. Ensuring you get that quality time for the entire family is number one.

Number two, another thing I see lacking in many situations with families is "parent" time. Parents have to have quality time, too. You have to have that time with your spouse and them to do things together. Not with the kids or other couples, just quality time for the two of you so that you can continue to enjoy your relationship.

This is key because these are some of the examples for your child. Being a parent, you are the ultimate role model. If you never go out with your spouse or do something together, then your kids aren't going to see that relationship. What starts to happen, especially if it is an only child situation, is that the child begins to think the world revolves around them because everything you do involves them, and your spouse does the same thing. That is not healthy for your child. They need to see the two of you interacting and enjoying each other.

If you are a single parent, this same rule applies. Obviously, instead of having "significant other" time, you will have your "alone" time.

*"Hey, Mom's going out tonight,"*

or if you are a father,

*"Dad is going out tonight."*

Showing the kids that you have a life outside of them so that they start to see what is expected as you get older.

Number three is "Alone" time. Even if you are in a nuclear family situation with a spouse and maybe even an extended family with grandparents, each parent should take their alone time.

Sometimes, mom doesn't have a job outside the home and stays with the kids all day. Dad comes home tired and wants to spend only a little time with the kids. He wants to watch TV or something. That starts to wear pretty thin very quickly. Mom deserves a break and some "alone" time if she wants.

Each parent needs to have their activity or thing to do so that they can get out of the house. Even if it is an hour, a half hour, a half day, or a full day, do something that you enjoy doing tak, take a break, and be able to come back more well-balanced and ready to be part of the family.

## ASSIGNMENT #12

A happy life is all about balance. When you are out of balance, you feel stress and unhappiness. Look at your routines - work, home, family, and self. Are all four of these in balance with each other? Most of the time, the answer will be "No." At least _ONE_ of these will be out of balance and require more attention. The point is to get as close as you can to perfect balance. That means making sure to spend quality time with your children. It does not have to be a huge vacation or expensive event. The fact that you are making memories with them is the most important.

Create a list of quality time events you would like to do with your children, ask them what things they think should be on the list, and then pull out your calendar and schedule them as best as you can.

Would you like to get free updates and some _COOL_ gifts?

I am constantly working on new skills and adding techniques to my toolkit. You will get it for free when I add something to this book. Just visit:

**http://DennyStrecker.com/confidencebook-bonus**

# 13

# FAMILY MEETING

*"Family is not an important thing. It's everything."*

— MICHAEL J. FOX

## THE TWO DOGS

A man had two Dogs: a Hound, trained to assist him in sports, and a House dog, taught to watch the house. He always gave the House dog a large share of his spoil when he returned home after a good day's sport. The Hound, feeling much aggrieved at this, reproached his companion, saying, "It is tough to have all this labor while you, who do not assist in the chase, luxuriate on the fruits of my exertions." The House dog replied, "Do not blame me, my friend, but find fault with the Master, who has not taught me to labor but to depend for subsistence on the labor of others.

## THE FAMILY MEETING

This is one thing that I don't see at all but that every family should be doing every week. You should have a weekly family meeting.

By having this weekly meeting, you are teaching your children that they are part of a group or team. We go through things together; we watch each other's back, support each other, and want to know what is going on in each other's lives. This meeting will change or evolve depending on the kids' age. If you have a toddler, they can, and should, still be involved in the meeting, but their input could be more significant if you have a teenager.

Here is how the meeting works. You sit down and ask,

*"What's going on in this upcoming week? This is what we have scheduled. This is what we have planned. We are doing this, and here are some things we would like to do."*

Lay out your calendar of events. Start showing your children this time management skill; they will benefit from it for a lifetime. In many cases, this may be the parents' first use of this skill, too. What a great experience for the entire family to share.

This can be tough for some parents, and that is okay. I am asked pretty often,

*"How do I teach my child self-confidence if I don't have self-confidence?"*

The answer is you can't. It would help if you worked on all of these skills that we are working on and then be able to pass them on to your children by demonstration and role modeling.

With your family meetings, you are going to work on your time management; you are going to lay out your schedule and be able to talk about vacations;

*"Hey, what are we going to do?*

*Where do you guys want to go this summer?*

*What is one thing you would like to do this Saturday?*

*Hey, we have got to clean the garage. When are we going to do that?*

*Who will take care of the backyard, mowing, or snow removal?"*

It is different from what is said, but it is essential that everybody is at the table and everybody contributes to the conversation.

You are learning to work as a family unit, spend more quality time together, and keep in touch with what is going on in everybody's life.

## ASSIGNMENT #13

Hosting a Family Meeting is a big deal and goes a long way to making everyone in the family feel like they are a part of it. Follow the steps described above and schedule your meeting as soon as possible. You will be happy that you did.

Would you like to get free updates and some _COOL_ gifts?

I am constantly working on new skills and adding techniques to my toolkit. You will get it for free when I add something to this book. Just visit:

**http://DennyStrecker.com/confidencebook-bonus**

# 14

# TEACH RESPECT

*"I'm not concerned with your liking or disliking me...*

*All I ask is that you respect me as a human being."*

— JACKIE ROBINSON

## THE LIONESS

A controversy prevailed among the beasts of the field as to which of the animals deserved the most credit for producing the most significant number of whelps at birth. They rushed clamorously into the presence of the Lioness and demanded of her the dispute settlement.

"And you," they said, "how many sons have you at birth?' The Lioness laughed at them and said:

"Why! I have only one, but that one is altogether a thorough-bred Lion."

## BE THE ROLE MODEL OF RESPECT.

One of my goals with this book is to spread the word to as many households as possible that the number one rule in this household is,

"No yelling in the house, period. We don't raise our voices; we don't cry and scream. We talk like people, and we talk with respect. If you are yelling and screaming, all respect has gone out the window. Parents tend to yell at their kids. While there is a time and place when raising your voice can be effective, too many parents use it as their first form of discipline. No yelling in the house means just that - no crying. There is no yelling in the house for the kids.

Remember, you must be a role model and use the skills you want your children to learn. You can take it to the extreme in this case, too. Let's say you are downstairs, the kids are upstairs, and you scream upstairs for them, "Hey, it's dinnertime!" That is yelling in the house, and that is not acceptable. You walk up the stairs, get the kids, or have one child get another child if you have multiple kids in the family and vice versa. If your kids want to talk to you, they should not yell down the stairs or from another room.

Another way you can apply this rule is if you are talking to me, then you need to have eye contact with me and ensure I have it with you. That way, I know you are talking to me. Too often, a young student will come to class and be super excited to tell me something they did that day. They will jump right into their story without getting my attention. Then, a couple of things can happen: either I did not hear the story because I was focused on something else, or they get hurt because they see I am not paying attention. Get eye contact first, and then I would love to hear your story.

Parents need to remember about this a lot of times. It is not going to click automatically. It is going to take some conscious effort, and it is going to take work on your part.

When you start to teach respect, think about how you like to be treated. Look at the way you are treating others and the things that you say to people. For example, somebody cuts you off on the road, and you swear or let some words go that you shouldn't. Well, that is teaching your child. Read the poem "Children learn what they live."

Available on the bonus website I created for you. If they see you doing that, they will think that it is how you deal with things - yell and scream when something doesn't go the right way for you.

## ASSIGNMENT #14

Think of what respect means to you and what it looks like. Then, set out to be the best role model of that behavior that you can be. You will be surprised at how quickly your children notice **AND** begin to mimic your behavior.

Would you like to get free updates and some _COOL_ gifts?

I am constantly working on new skills and adding techniques to my toolkit. You will get it for free when I add something to this book. Just visit:

**http://DennyStrecker.com/confidencebook-bonus**

# 15

# LEARN SOMETHING NEW

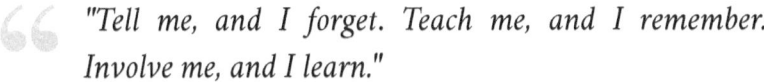

*"Tell me, and I forget. Teach me, and I remember. Involve me, and I learn."*

— BENJAMIN FRANKLIN

## THE WIDOW AND THE SHEEP

A certain poor widow had one solitary Sheep. At shearing time, wishing to take his fleece and avoid the expense, she sheared him herself but used the shears so unskillfully that she clipped the flesh with the fleece. The Sheep, writhing with pain, said, "Why do you hurt me so, Mistress? What weight can my blood add to the wool? If you want my flesh, there is the butcher, who will kill me in an instant; but if you want my fleece and wool, there is the shearer, who will shear and not hurt me.

## HAVE YOUR CHILD TEACH YOU

A great way to spend some of that quality time (from the previous chapter) is to have them teach you a particular activity. This is huge for their self-confidence. Getting them to the point where they know something that you don't and they can share that knowledge will make them feel great about themselves.

Their self-confidence and their self-esteem is going to skyrocket at that point. Does everything they show you have to be absolutely 100% correct? No, it never does. The idea is you have them teaching it to you.

If you want it to be the latest video game, you say to your child,

*"Teach me how to play this game or get to this level."*

Or,

*"Hey, what were you doing in school this week?"*

*"We worked on adding and subtracting."*

*"Well, great. It's been a long time since I have done that.*

*I could have improved my math skills in school.*

*Can you teach me?"*

Have them teach you, and then, at that point, you are saying,

"Hey. Wow, that was great. I forgot all about that one point. You showed me something new, thank you very much."

Again, it does not matter what the activity is, but having your child teach you how to do it will give them that massive boost in self-confidence.

## ASSIGNMENT #15

Make it a point to learn something you are interested in and would like to know more about. It could be woodcarving, model building, insects, or a language. It does not matter what it is, as long as you find it interesting.

Then, learn as much as possible about it and enjoy the process.

Would you like to get free updates and some _COOL_ gifts?

I am constantly working on new skills and adding techniques to my toolkit. You will get it for free when I add something to this book. Just visit:

**http://DennyStrecker.com/confidencebook-bonus**

# 16

# THINKING POSITIVE

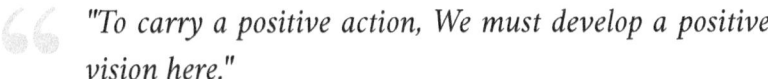 *"To carry a positive action, We must develop a positive vision here."*

— DALAI LAMA

## THE HUNTER AND THE WOODMAN

A hunter, not very bold, was searching for the tracks of a Lion. He asked a man felling oaks in the forest if he had seen any marks of his footsteps or knew where his lair was. "I will," said the man, "at once show you the Lion himself." Turning very pale and chattering with his teeth from fear, the Hunter replied, "No, thank you. I did not ask that; it is his track only I am in search of, not the Lion himself.

## THINKING POSITIVE

One of the challenges I give parents with children in my program is removing negative words from their vocabulary. One of the things we talk about specifically is removing the word "no" from your vocabulary. To be clear, I am not telling you never to tell your child "no." We will say "no" to them all the time because we have rules and consequences in place. Success comes in how to say "no" without using the word "no."

For example, a seven-year-old approached me while his mom stood behind him. She surprised me with this meeting because she did not let me know anything about the issue ahead of time. I guess the child wanted to quit karate, and it was just about time for class to start, so what I think happened is,

Child: *"I don't want to go; I want to quit."*

Mom: *"Okay, Mom says go talk to Shihan"* (which is my title, master teacher), and she says, *"Well, go talk to Shihan, and if he says okay, then we will quit."*

She could say that because she knows I am never going to say,

*"Well, yeah. Okay, fine. You can quit."*

The child comes up to me and says,

*"Shihan. I want to quit karate,"*

I say, *"Sure, you can quit once you earn your Black Belt."*

He says, *"Okay, great."*

At this point, he turns around, walks away, starts getting his shoes, and thinks he is done. Now, granted, because he was not listening very clearly and he is used to just being told yes or no, he did not understand. Kids are used to hearing the word "no" all the time, so they ask five or six times to see if they can get through it.

Changing the conversation with

him, I did two things. I was able to teach the parent how to say "no" without saying "no," and, at the same time, I was able to stop the student,

*"Did you hear what I said?"*

*"Yeah, you said I could quit."*

*"That's not what I said. I said you could quit when you earned your Black Belt. What belt are you in right now?" "Well, I'm a Blue Belt,"*

*"Okay. Well, then, you have got several more belts. Go get out on the floor."*

He looked at me briefly, took off his shoes, went out on the floor, and had a great class.

One of the essential things to understand is that children are present-minded until around twelve years old. This explains a common complaint I hear from parents,

"Well, my kid doesn't want to come to karate class, but once they're here, they have a great time."

Well, absolutely. I can tell you precisely what is happening. They are either playing with their friends, playing their favorite video game, or watching a cartoon, and the parent comes in and says,

*"Okay, it's time to go to karate. Let's go."*

No matter how much fun your child has at karate, that does not matter. They do not remember all of the fun times. They are sitting there doing their favorite thing right now; they do not want to leave it.

By using this skill and knowing that kids are present-minded, they only think about the one thing they are doing right now. By being two or three steps ahead of them, you can guide them to the decision in the process that you want. Have the kids do something that they do not enjoy doing before any activity that they do enjoy. Then, when you say it is time to do the next thing, they will be excited to do it.

I am getting back into thinking positively and being able to remove negative words. The first step to creating any habit is to catch yourself using negative words and be able to replace them.

A classic example I use is when people say, "I have to."

*"Well, why don't you play, Daddy?"*

*"Well, because I have to go to work."*

Again, subconsciously, what you are doing now is you are teaching your kids that work is terrible because you HAVE to do it. Work is alright. Work pays the bills. It is not that I HAVE to go to work; I get to work.

*"Well, I **GET** to go to work because that is what gives us this nice house, gives us food on the table, and allows us to spend our quality time together."*

Now, this is a big challenge because many people hate their job. If you fall into that category, then there are other issues that you need to address.

I am not condoning that you start lying to your child and saying how great work is. Still, at the same time, they don't need to know that your boss or manager is the worst manager in the world or whatever other adjectives you use to describe your work. That is not their business. Being grateful that you have a job and something that brings in money is all the kids need to know now. Then, as they get older, you can teach them the other things about work.

If you find yourself in a situation where you are not sure how to spin it and get out of removing the word "no" or how to change it to a positive sentence, by all means, send me an e-mail. I love those little challenges and want to see what we can put together for your situation.

## ASSIGNMENT #16

Are you a positive person? Do you think and speak positively? You have to learn how to if you want your child to do it. This ties back into role modeling the behavior you want to see. Keep track of what you say and how you act for a few days and see if you lean towards the negative or the positive.

If you lean towards the negative, you have got to change your thinking so you can change your language.

Would you like to get free updates and some _COOL_ gifts?

I am constantly working on new skills and adding techniques to my toolkit. You will get it for free when I add something to this book. Just visit:

**http://DennyStrecker.com/confidencebook-bonus**

# 17

# TEACH THE VALUE MONEY

*"Money won't create success, the freedom to make it will."*

— NELSON MANDELA

### THE TWO FROGS

Two Frogs were neighbors. One inhabited a deep pond, far removed from public view; the other lived in a gully containing little water and traversed by a country road. The Frog that lived in the pond warned his friend to change his residence and implored him to come and live with him, saying that he would enjoy greater safety from danger and more abundant food. The other refused, saying that he felt it so very hard to leave a place to which he had become accustomed. A few days afterward, a heavy wagon passed through the gully and crushed him to death under its wheels.

## TEACH THE VALUE OF MONEY

It can be tough to teach the value of money sometimes because some adults struggle with it. They live on credit cards and have way too much debt. They are working as much as possible to reduce their debt but end up just spinning their wheels. Or worse, get farther and farther behind no matter how hard they try.

If you have a lot of debt, you can still teach your child the value of money. Are you role-modeling a particular lifestyle that you cannot afford? If so, they will be inclined to pick up that bad habit. There is a big difference between being in debt and working your way out of it and being in debt and wallowing in it. Working your way out will teach your child good habits. Wallowing will not.

Everybody's situation is different, so we could discuss and work on many things here. For a basic start, do you give your child an allowance? This would be one place to start. I am not condoning if you do or if you don't; that is certainly a specific family choice. If you give an allowance, I recommend you start taking 10% or 15% and teaching your kids about taxes. You write it out just like you see on your paychecks. You have federal and state withholding; sometimes, you have city with-holding and Social Security.

Now, the more important fact is what you do with that money. What I recommend is to set that money aside. You put it into a separate account without telling the kids. Then, whatever landmark in their life comes along, maybe their 18th birthday or whatever situation you want. You give them that money back,

"Here is all the money we took as taxes from your allowance growing up."

At that point, "Hey, they will buy a car. They are going to buy this or that big item." Then, you can help them out by giving them that extra cash.

Indeed, teaching them that you don't get 100% of what you earn will be important. Another skill to develop is to be able to compare money to time. Everything in this world either costs you money or time.

It doesn't get any simpler than that. One of the things that I was looking at several years ago was having my house painted. Well, I had two choices:

#1 - I can either do it myself, and it is going to take me two to three weeks to do it over multiple days and weekends

**Or**

#2 - I can pay somebody to come in and do it, and they will get them done in one or two days.

I have to invest my time or my money. So, there is no right or wrong answer. It is up to me to decide which is more valuable.

Another concept parents can teach their children is how to barter.

"Hey, you want this item or this toy? OK. Well, then, you have to do this chore."

That allows them to think and decide whether the offer is worth it.

This would be an additional chore, not one that they are already responsible for, but that will take their time. It could be raking the leaves in the backyard or cleaning the basement. Make sure this is age-specific and appropriate.

You want to teach them to think and say,

"OK. Well, I have to invest my time because I don't have money,"

and then equate that with money, then you can save some time. If you don't have money, well then you have to take and invest more time.

## ASSIGNMENT #17

Look for opportunities to teach your child about money and what things cost. Let them know that things are not FREE and that they don't just GET anything they want anytime they want it.

I have created a job list that you can download to give some ideas on how to set up a system like this for your family.

Would you like to get free updates and some COOL gifts?

I am constantly working on new skills and adding techniques to my toolkit. You will get it for free when I add something to this book. Just visit:

**http://DennyStrecker.com/confidencebook-bonus**

# 18

# LEARN RESPONSIBILITY

*"Hold yourself responsible for a higher standard than anybody expects of you. Never excuse yourself."*

— HENRY WARD BEECHER

## THE BAT AND THE WEASELS

Bat, who fell upon the ground and was caught by a Weasel, pleaded to be spared his life. The Weasel refused, saying that he was, by nature, the enemy of all birds. The Bat assured him that he was not a bird but a mouse and thus was set free. Shortly afterward, the Bat again fell to the ground and was caught by another Weasel, whom he likewise entreated not to eat him. The Weasel said that he had a special hostility to mice. The Bat assured him that he was not a mouse but a bat, and thus a second time escaped.

### Responsibility

Teaching your child to be responsible is one of the biggest reasons parents bring their children to me. How many times have you said to yourself as a parent,

"I wish my child would be more responsible."

As parents, we want our children to grow up being responsible. That includes taking responsibility for their actions, commitments, outcomes, and decisions.

When your child was born, you assumed full responsibility for them. Then, over the next 18 years, your job is to gradually turn that responsibility back to them by teaching them how to take care of themselves. Teaching your child to be responsible takes time and attention; every bit of responsibility you give your child must come with tremendous instruction and supervision. To raise a responsible child, you must be prepared to teach, remind, and inspect over a zillion times if necessary. Preparing to do it without becoming frustrated, impatient, or resentful would be best.

What we have is a model that you can follow to teach your child how to handle responsibility. There are four basic steps:

#1 - You assign a task, and you teach what you expect and how to meet those expectations.

#2 - You provide an opportunity to work on that particular task.

#3 - You inspect, and you provide constructive feedback. The emphasis needs to be on the constructive feedback.

#4 - Reach your goal. Celebrate and set a new goal.

Too often, parents talk sarcastically to their kids. When they turn into teenagers, and they have heard that for the past 12 to 15 years, and it starts coming back at you, it is going to be razor sharp, and it is going to be polished, and it is going to be very difficult to deal with. You teach that skill to them if you speak to them that way.

The next point I want you to think about is not using the word "but" in sentences. Anytime somebody uses the word "but," it means,

"Ignore what I've said before. Here is my excuse for not doing it."

If you give your child a particular task and then you say,

"Well, that looks good, but if you do this, it'll be better."

There is nothing constructive; it is just harmful. Your child is not going to remember you said it looks good. They are only going to remember that you were not happy. Remove the word "but" and make it constructive criticism.

OK, back to our model. What do you do when your child is not successful? You continue with step number three, going back with constructive criticism. If your child's results were not entirely successful, you go back to Step #1. You assign the task and teach what you expect and how to meet those expectations.

Don't throw in the towel and say,

"Forget it, I'll do it myself."

If you do, you are destroying your child's self-confidence and self-esteem. You are telling them that you don't believe in them or that they can do the task correctly. That is NEVER a message you want to send to your child.

Start to implement the responsibility model today. Don't take away the responsibility if your child's efforts were unsuccessful. It just means your child needs more teaching and more feedback. You must be patient and supportive. Your child will become discouraged and resentful if you appear disappointed or impatient.

If you don't have a responsible child, think about it. Some parents say,

"OK, yeah. They are five, they are seven, they are 10, they are not responsible. So what?"

How many stories do you hear about adults still living at home at 30 years old, 35 years old, or older? They have never been able to go out and live alone because they are not responsible enough.

I don't know any parent that has a child saying,

"You know what? I'm looking forward to when my child is 40 and still in the house."

As much as you love them and as much as you want them to be part of your life, you want them to be able to stand on their own two feet.

Being able to teach them responsibility is going to be necessary. Still, it is a huge mistake to assume that children will become responsible adults without coaching and help. You have got to be diligent, use this model, don't become frustrated or give up. Giving up is not an option. If you stick with it, your child will learn to handle all types of responsibility effectively.

It is not always straightforward because you will catch yourself forgetting or using those negative words. That is OK. When you forget, make sure you catch it the next time. If you become negative, stop, breathe, and change your vocabulary. Strive for improvement, not perfection. Does that sound familiar?

## ASSIGNMENT #18

One of the greatest gifts you can give your child is the ability to be responsible. As with all valuable things, this skill must be taught to children until they get it. That means over and over again for months or even years.

Create a Responsibility List. This is a list of things you want your child to be able to do on their own. Next, number each item in order of preference. What is the #1 thing in your opinion that your child needs to learn? Then #2, #3, and so on. Now, go back to number #1 and plan how you will teach that skill to your child. In our previous chapter, a great place to start would be having the kids make their beds.

You can make the list as long as you like. Here are some of the things I think are essential:

- Cleaning your room.
- Picking up after yourself.

- Using a vacuum.
- Doing laundry, how to make breakfast.
- Getting your own beverages.
- Getting your own snacks, how to cook.
- Managing money and getting up every morning on time.

This is not a complete list, but it is enough to keep you busy for a few years.

Would you like to get free updates and some COOL gifts?

I am constantly working on new skills and adding techniques to my toolkit. You will get it for free when I add something to this book. Just visit:

**http://DennyStrecker.com/confidencebook-bonus**

# 19

# GIVE UNCONDITIONAL LOVE

 *"Being deeply loved by someone gives you strength while loving someone deeply gives you courage."*

— LAO TZU

## THE LION AND THE THREE BULLS

Three bulls pastured together for a long time. A Lion lay in ambush, hoping to make them his prey, but was afraid to attack them while they kept together. Having finally succeeded in separating them by guileful speeches, he attacked them without fear as they fed alone and feasted on them one by one at his leisure.

**Unconditional Love**

Giving unconditional love is both verbal and physical. You hear people all of the time say,

"My parents never told me that they loved me."

**Or,**

"They never hugged me; our family are not huggers."

That is a crime. All right, I may be biased. I am huge about giving out hugs to people - especially if they are having a bad day. Anybody that asks me for one can certainly get it. I am more than happy to oblige for a couple of reasons. First, it just gives the person that sense that I care - which I do. Second, it releases a hormone called Oxytocin (the "love hormone") in both the other person AND me. So it makes it a win-win event because we both feel happier now!

There is so much power in a hug. I was watching the movie "Santa Clause 3" one night. It wasn't a great movie, so you don't have to rent it immediately. At the end of the movie, the little girl gives Jack Frost (who is obviously Mr. Cold) a hug, which warms him up and changes his whole life. So, seeing stuff like that is very powerful.

So, if you are not a hugger, try to start. It can be a pat on the back, a high five, or even a handshake. Any personal contact is a good start and will release more Oxytocin into your system. So, hugging is what works for me, and it is what I enjoy. If it works for you, great! If not, find something else that works.

The two most important things about this process are

#1 - Tell your children, your spouse, your family, and your friends how important they are to you, and tell them that you love them, and tell them regularly. Not just once in a while.

#2 - Show it and make it physical. If it is a high five or a hug, whatever works for you is fine. Find your thing.

## ASSIGNMENT #19

I have created a worksheet of 100 Ways to Reinforce Your Child Positively. You can download this worksheet at my bonus website listed below. Then, work on using all 100 phrases or sayings, and see how long it takes. Then start again and try to beat your best time.

Would you like to get free updates and some COOL gifts?

I am constantly working on new skills and adding techniques to my toolkit. You will get it for free when I add something to this book. Just visit:

**http://DennyStrecker.com/confidencebook-bonus**

# ACTIVELY LISTEN

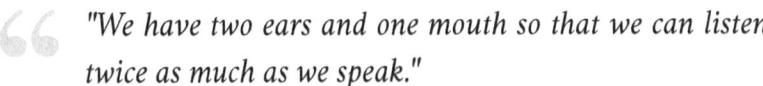
*"We have two ears and one mouth so that we can listen twice as much as we speak."*

— EPICTETUS

## THE NORTH WIND AND THE SUN

The North Wind and the Sun disputed as to which was the most powerful and agreed that he should be declared the victor who could first strip a wayfaring man of his clothes. The North Wind first tried his power and blew with all his might, but the keener his blasts, the closer the Traveler wrapped his cloak around him, until at last, resigning all hope of victory, the Wind called upon the Sun to see what he could do. The Sun suddenly shone out with all his warmth. The Traveler no sooner felt his genial rays than he took off one garment after another and, at last, fairly overcome with heat, undressed and bathed in a stream that lay in his path.

## Actively Listen

Actively listening to your child is an important skill to develop so they know that you are paying attention to them and what they are saying. Parents too often say,

"Yeah, yep, uh-huh, OK, great." Etc.

Instead, look at your child, eye to eye, when they are talking. If you ever watch me working with kids, you will first notice that I squat down to their level because I want to connect with them. I do not like a child looking up at me when they talk. That puts me in a position of superiority. It makes me look big and scary. I do not want to look big and scary to any child. I want them to feel happy and safe around me, so I do everything possible to create that atmosphere.

So make sure you squat down to your child's level so you can make eye contact with them while they are talking. They may be shy, look down, or look away. That is telling you that they lack confidence in themselves. Start to create opportunities for them to practice making eye contact. If you see your child is not looking at you, you can say something like,

"Hey! Look at this?" and then make the silliest face you can.

Do something like that enough times, and your child will WANT to look at you to see what you might do next.

I always get kids running into my karate school to tell me something they did that day. They wanted to share it with me, and if I took those two seconds to stop whatever I was doing and speak to them, it made their day. Whatever they have to tell me probably is not "earth-shattering," but it means the world to that child, so it is important to me.

You need to take the time, even if it is just two seconds or even if it is 10 minutes, to listen actively. Give them good eye contact and your undivided attention. Then, ask them questions or add to their story, and you will watch them light up like crazy.

## ASSIGNMENT #20

Start to participate in conversations with your child. Ask them questions about what they are telling you so they can tell you even more about it. You can score "cool" points by adding something to their story and letting them run with it.

It is easy to get bogged down with the day-to-day stuff and forget that your child NEEDS your attention. But by giving them just a few minutes of your time each day, they will be happy for a lifetime.

Go ask your child right now, "What are you doing?"

Would you like to get free updates and some COOL gifts?

I am constantly working on new skills and adding techniques to my toolkit. You will get it for free when I add something to this book. Just visit:

**http://DennyStrecker.com/confidencebook-bonus**

# 21

# MAKING EVERY EXPERIENCE A LESSON IN LEARNING

 *"There are no secrets to success. It is the result of preparation, hard work, and learning from failure."*

— COLIN POWELL

## THE FISHERMAN

Some Fishermen were out trawling their nets. Perceiving them to be very heavy, they danced about for joy and supposed that they had taken a large catch. When they had dragged the nets to the shore, they found but few fish: the nets were full of sand and stones, and the men were beyond measure cast down so much at the disappointment which had befallen them, but because they had formed such very different expectations. One of their company, an old man, said, "Let us cease lamenting, my mates, for, as it seems to me, sorrow is always the twin sister of joy, and it was only to be looked for that we, who just now were over-rejoiced, should next have something to make us sad.

## Lesson Learned

Parents should make every situation a positive learning experience. It is so easy to be negative, yell, scream, put down, or punish. When that happens, you miss an opportunity to help your child learn something.

OK, you messed up.

So what?

All right, please fix it. Here is how. By making it into a learning experience, you will increase the chances that this does not happen again. If you yell and scream at them, it will probably happen again. It is just a matter of when. That is because children forget, and when they forget, they make the same silly mistake again.

That can be tough. If you are in the heat of the moment, and your child s just done something, you may yell at them. I remember computers and the internet just came out when I was young. My dad worked for IBM. He had just spent hours and hours working on the computer connected to the phone line. He told us not to pick up the phone, but I forgot. I picked up the phone to make a call, and the phone connection was lost. He lost all the work he had done for the past two hours. He was not pleased. He yelled at me for quite a while.

How can you make something a positive learning experience? Take your time, step back, and take a deep breath. Then, say to your child;

"OK, I'm very upset. Let me calm down before we talk about this."

Nothing says that you have to discipline and work with your child right away. Try to find a positive solution.

## ASSIGNMENT #21

Make it a point to find opportunities to teach your child something. If you stay on the lookout, you will begin to see how many there are in a day. It could be to explain WHY something is done this way or that way. It could be teaching them something they did not know about. It may be a chance to ask them questions. It does not matter WHAT the opportunity is; just make sure you take it.

Would you like to get free updates and some COOL gifts?

I am constantly working on new skills and adding techniques to my toolkit. You will get it for free when I add something to this book. Just visit:

**http://DennyStrecker.com/confidencebook-bonus**

# 22

# BECOME AN EXPERT

 *"An investment in knowledge pays the best interest.."*

— BENJAMIN FRANKLIN

## HERCULES AND THE WAGONER

A carter was driving a wagon along a country lane when the wheels sank deep into a rut. The rustic driver, stupefied and aghast, stood looking at the wagon and did nothing but utter loud cries to Hercules to come and help him. Hercules, it is said, appeared and thus addressed him: "Put your shoulders to the wheels, my man. Goad on your bullocks, and never more pray to me for help, until you have done your best to help yourself or depend upon it, you will henceforth pray in vain.

## BE THE EXPERT

What I mean by becoming an expert is to get involved in what your kids are doing. A lot of activities have what I call "drop off" parents. Parents will drop their kids off and then say,

"OK, they are in class, great. I have an hour so that I can do something else."

Occasionally, this may be necessary, especially if you have more than one child. But some parents do this every class - day in, day out, week after week, month after month. They have no idea what their child is doing, what they are learning, or the benefits they get from the activity.

Don't be that type of parent! Get involved in what your kids are doing. Become a part of it, and then become the "expert" so that you can help them when they need it. You can also spend quality time with them because you can answer their questions and help.

A great example is homework. Parents all the time say,

"I can't help you with Algebra because I always stunk at it. I was terrible."

Well, you have a child now. It is time to get good at it. You have a second chance, so sit down with them and learn algebra or whatever the subject might be. Become an expert so your child sees you as the "go-to" source for the answers.

## ASSIGNMENT #22

Start with a single subject. Is your child into Minecraft or Skylanders? Learn about the game, the characters, the goals, etc., so you can participate in the conversation. Why not even play the game a little? Let them teach you how to play so THEY can feel like the expert.

Would you like to get free updates and some COOL gifts?

I am constantly working on new skills and adding techniques to my toolkit. You will get it for free when I add something to this book. Just visit:

**http://DennyStrecker.com/confidencebook-bonus**

# 23

# LEAD A HEALTHY LIFESTYLE

## THE ANTS AND THE GRASSHOPPER

The Ants spent a fine winter's day drying grain collected in the summertime. A Grasshopper, perishing with famine, passed by and earnestly begged for a little food. The Ants asked him, "Why did you not treasure up food during the summer?' He replied, "I had not leisure enough. I passed the days in singing." They then said in derision: "If you were foolish enough to sing all the summer, you must dance supperless to bed in the winter.

## HEALTHY LIFESTYLE

Parents need to teach their children how to have a healthy life-style. I have added a couple of stories to the bonus website for you to read. Obesity is a big problem today. It is reaching epidemic proportions.

Let me give you two rules to help you keep your child moving and active - especially during summer.

The first rule is:

Reading time should equal TV, video games, or computer time.

If your child wants to watch TV for an hour, no problem. They need to read a book for an hour. If they're going to spend all day Saturday in front of the TV, then they need to spend all day some other day reading a book. By setting these limits, you will get rid of those couch potatoes.

Does it have to be reading time? No. If you have a young child, it could be playtime. It would be best to be outside playing for every minute you are inside watching TV. So you can tweak this to fit your child's needs.

"Well, I'm not watching TV. I'm playing on my new WII, PlayStation, or Nintendo."

That's TV time.

"But I'm playing on the computer/tablet."

Anything with a screen is TV time.

The second rule for your children, and you as a matter of fact because you are a role model for your children, is that they should go to bed at the same time every day, seven days a week, 365 days a year, and should also get up at the same time every day of the year.

Why is this important?

You and your children are going to get a lot more done. Can you imagine how many Saturdays and Sundays are wasted by your teenagers sleeping until 1:00 pm? I hear this all the time. My martial arts class for the kids is at 11:00 am and 12:00 pm, and I get sleepy eyes walking in the door because their parents pulled them out of bed to come to karate at noon.

I am up at 8:00 am and at the school by 9:00 to prepare for classes. So I have been up for hours, and I have gotten a lot of things done.

That is a goal; it is not a rule; there is a difference. Your goal is to do this every day of the year. If you miss one, is that OK? Absolutely! We are not perfect; we are human beings. So you want to find a happy medium and get back on track as soon as possible.

## ASSIGNMENT #23

Start to find ways to improve your lifestyle for the entire family. Make a list and decide which item is the most important to start and do just that one. Then, move on to the next when you believe the first one is solid and in place.

Would you like to get free updates and some COOL gifts?

I am constantly working on new skills and adding techniques to my toolkit. You will get it for free when I add something to this book. Just visit:

**http://DennyStrecker.com/confidencebook-bonus**

# 24

# GIVE YOUR CHILD CHORES

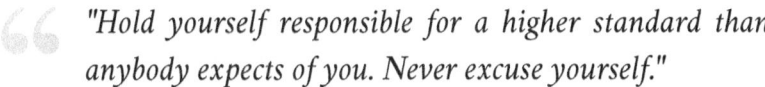

*"Hold yourself responsible for a higher standard than anybody expects of you. Never excuse yourself."*

— HENRY WARD BEECHER

## THE TRAVELER AND HIS DOG

A traveler about to embark on a journey saw his Dog stand at the door stretching himself. He asked him sharply: "Why do you stand there gaping? Everything is ready but you, so come with me instantly." The Dog, wagging his tail, replied: "O, master! I am quite ready; it is you for whom I am waiting.

## YOUR CHILD SHOULD HAVE CHORES

Every family I see where the children do not have chores is a family in struggle. Again, the children start to feel that they owe everything and that the world revolves around them, and I can see why.

Suppose you look back in the ancient Egyptian times with the pharaohs or any history where there was a king or a monarch of any sort, and they waited on hand and foot. In that case, there becomes a sense of entitlement. Why wouldn't kids pick that up? If I can yell downstairs, "Mom, get me a soda!" and you bring it to him, you'll start creating that situation. Indeed, make sure, again, that chores are age-appropriate, and at that point, you have to decide on what you think is appropriate.

Again, we've got two schools of thought. You've got some of the parents that would fall more on the hardcore, a military side, and so at that point, it becomes they're very strict, and it's got to be done precisely this way or else it's wrong. Then, you've got the exact opposite: "Well, it's easier for me to do it than them, so I'm not going to bother giving them any chores because it'll take twice as long." After I get done smacking you upside the head with that thinking, basically, what you're getting to or what I try to approach is you want short-term pain for long-term gain.

I would instead work with a child at whatever age now for three to six months to teach them this particular habit, whatever that habit might be, which is going to last the rest of their life rather than ignore it and have to do this extra work and extra task myself for the next five, 10, 15 years. Then, at that point, once they move out on their own, they're still not going to have that skill, so they're still coming back and trying to rely on it. A perfect example is when kids go off to college. We all joke about it here, at least in the United States.

When kids go out to college, they come home for two things, well, sometimes three, but basically: money and, more important, laundry. I don't know any college students, and I'm sure they're out there; I just haven't met them yet who haven't come home with that big massive bag of dirty clothes that says, "Great, I'm home. Here, do my laundry." Even if you don't do it, if they bring it home and they do it themselves, that's one step better. Indeed, if you start young, give the kids or your children just a small chore.

Whether it's setting the table for dinner, emptying the dishwasher, putting your clothes in the clothes bin, or anything like that so that they realize that as part of this family, your responsibility is to take care of these chores, and we all have chores. Then, they know that the family is essential and that everybody participating as a group will strengthen the family.

## ASSIGNMENT #24

Create a list of chores for your child to complete each week. You can attach rewards for completed sheets if you like.

Would you like to get free updates and some COOL gifts?

I am constantly working on new skills and adding techniques to my toolkit. You will get it for free when I add something to this book. Just visit:

**http://DennyStrecker.com/confidencebook-bonus**

# PUTTING IT ALL TOGETHER

*"A leader knows the way, goes the way, and shows the way."*

— JOHN C. MAXWELL

## THE DOG AND THE SHADOW

A Dog, crossing a bridge over a stream with a piece of flesh in his mouth, saw his own shadow in the water and took it for that of another Dog, with a piece of meat double his own in size. He immediately let go of his own and fiercely attacked the other Dog to get his larger piece from him. Thus, he lost both that which he grasped in the water because it was a shadow and his own because the stream swept it away.

## WHERE DO I BEGIN?

It is easy to become overwhelmed with all of this information and end up not doing anything.

Don't let that happen!

Make it a point to add something to your parenting arsenal at least once a month. Be ready to stick with it for at least three weeks. 90% of people give up 10% away from their goal. Read that again...

Don't throw in the towel and fall into the trap where you say to yourself,

"This isn't working!"

If you hang in there, success is very likely around the next corner. You have to keep your eye on the goal and remain vigilant.

I approach each situation because I have two options:

#1 - I can continue to work on this situation, and the child will eventually get it.

#2 - Give up

#2 is NEVER an option to me. So, I continue to work and help the child however I can.

This mindset allows me to remain calm and not get frustrated because I know I am in it for the long haul. However long it takes. Because anything else is unfair to the child, I will always give every child my 100% best.

If you keep the end in mind, you will be better able to handle the short-term struggles that are bound to come up. Frustration develops when you lose sight of your goal and feel "stuck." Keep moving forward, even if it is just a crawl, to prevent yourself from feeling stuck. Stick to your guns, and you will be happy that you did.

## ASSIGNMENT #25

Take a deep breath, relax, and think about what you believe is the most important skill you want your child to learn. Then, go back, read that chapter again, and start there.

Just take one skill at a time and begin to implement it. After several weeks, pick the next and add that to your plan. Before you know it, you will see some positive results and want to keep going.

Would you like to get free updates and some COOL gifts?

I am constantly working on new skills and adding techniques to my toolkit. You will get it for free when I add something to this book. Just visit:

**http://DennyStrecker.com/confidencebook-bonus**

# ABOUT THE AUTHOR

Denny Strecker teaches children the Life Skills necessary to lead a happy and successful life so that their parents NEVER have to wonder or worry about them. He has helped thousands of children earn better grades, learn how to lead a group and set and reach goals others only dream about.

Denny has owned and operated his karate school for the past 25 years, which is located in Troy, Michigan. He has hundreds of students come to his classes weekly to work on their Life Skills and Development so they can do better in school and prepare for the real world.

Denny has spent the past 25 years studying child development and how to become the best teacher—thousands of hours studying neuroscience, age-specific training, age-appropriate development, and game theory.

He has used his classroom as his laboratory to see what things work (and what things don't work) hundreds of times to get the best results possible. Things that worked, he used again. Things that did not get thrown out. Today, he has the most effective teaching system available for children ages 4 to 15.

Denny is originally from Troy, Michigan, and it was a great day when he moved his karate school back to his hometown in 2014.

He has a Golden doodle named Yoshi, his best friend, and they hang out on the couch, watch movies, and spend a lot of time playing at the park.

You can get more information from the sources below:

YouTube: https://www.youtube.com/user/karatefit

Facebook: https://www.facebook.com/denny.strecker

Twitter: http://www.Twitter.com/DSKTroy

Blog: http://dennystrecker.com/

Website: https://PrestigeMartialArtsTroy.com

Amazon Author Page: http://www.amazon.com/author/dennystrecker

**HIRE DENNY TO SPEAK AT YOUR EVENT!**

Book Denny Strecker as your Keynote Speaker, and You're Guaranteed to Make Your Event Highly Entertaining and Unforgettable!

Denny Strecker has been educating, entertaining, and helping parents build and grow their skills to raise healthy and happy children for over two decades.

His story includes owning and operating his martial arts school since 1992, where he has been able to practice and develop the tools needed to help children grow into the best versions of themselves. He has found the "secrets" to getting children to listen better, focus, set and complete goals, and become leaders. After spending twenty-five years perfecting his skills, he is now sharing his best-kept "secrets" with his parents so they can benefit too.

His unique style inspires, empowers, and entertains audiences while giving them the tools and strategies they need and want to help their children develop into great adults.

For more info, visit www.DennyStrecker.com/ speaking or call (248) 687-8641.

# ONE LAST THING...

If you enjoyed this book or found it helpful, I would be grateful if you posted a short review on Amazon. Your support makes a difference, and I read all the reviews personally to get your feedback and make this book even better.

If you would like to leave a review, then all you need to do is click the review link on this book's page on Amazon here:

https://www.amazon.com/review/create-review/ref=
cm_cr_dp_d_wr_but_top?ie=UTF8&channel=glance-detail&
asin=B071XPBG46#

Thanks again for your support!